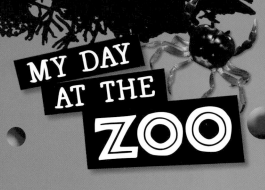

MY DAY AT THE ZOO

AMAZING AQUARIUM

Terry Jennings

QED Publishing

Consultant: Steve Parker
Editor: Eve Marleau
Designer and
Picture Researcher: Liz Wiffen

Copyright © QED Publishing 2010

First published in the UK in 2010 by
QED Publishing
A Quarto Group Company
226 City Road
London EC1V 2TT

www.qed-publishing.co.uk

ISBN 978 1 84835 395 4

Printed and bound in China

Picture credits Key: t=top, b=bottom, r=right,
l=left, c=centre
Alamy 13 WILDLIFE GmbH
NHPA 13b Norbert Wu, 21t Kevin Schafer
Photolibrary 4c Javier Larrea, 6b Poelzer
Poelzer, 7t Norbert Probst, 7b Reinhard Dirscherl,
8b Paul Kay, 9c Tobias Bernhard, 14t David B
Fleetham, 16c Paul Kay, 19t Peter Walton, 21b
Alberto Muro Pelliconi
Shutterstock 1t & folios Steffen Foerster
Photography, 1b bernd.neeser, 2b Eric Isselée,
3r Chen Wei Seng, 5t Eric Isselée, 8t Heather
L. Jones, 10l Chen Wei Seng, 11t Studio 37, 12b
kojik, 15t aida ricciardiello, 15b Geoff Hardy, 17t
Ivanova Inga, 18t PBorowka, 18b Tyler Fox, 20l
tubuceo, 21c kristian sekulic, 24b Eric Isselée
SPL 11b Paul Zahl
stock.xchange all pages (coral borders)
Swandieve & hirekatsu, 6t 11t 15b 18b porah, 5t
17b satty4u

The words in **bold** are explained
in the glossary on page 22.

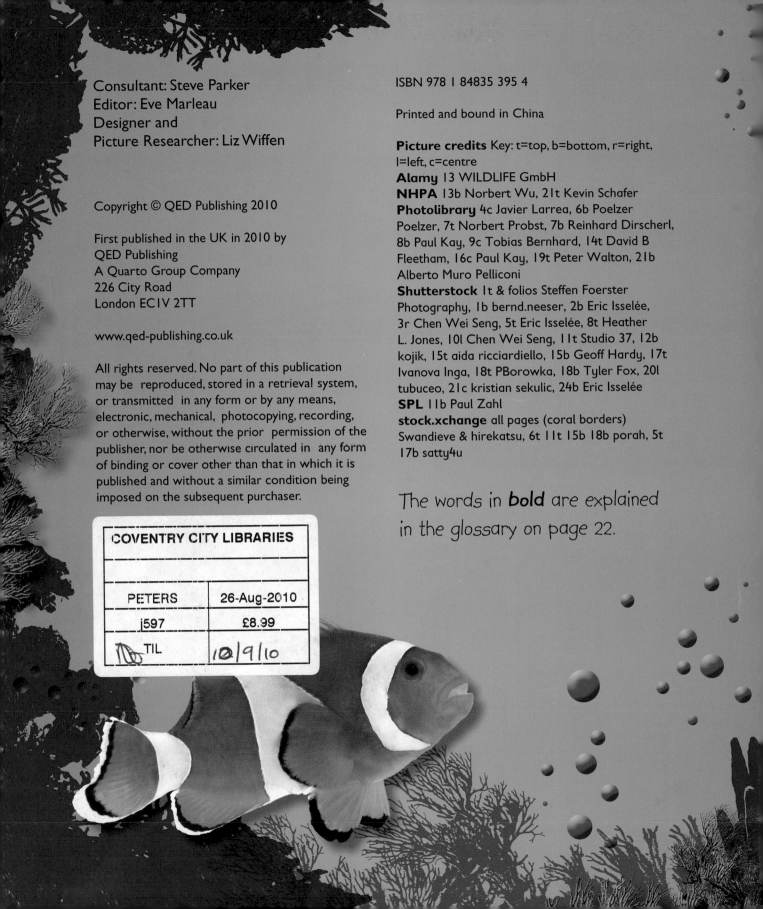

Contents

What is an aquarium?

We are going to an aquarium today. An aquarium is a large building containing tanks where fish and other water animals are kept for people to see.

↑ Aquariums often have tanks with many different kinds of fish.

Aquariums let you see lots of different fish and water animals from all over the world. They also **breed** creatures that are in danger of becoming **extinct**, or dying out. They work to protect the environments that these creatures live in, too.

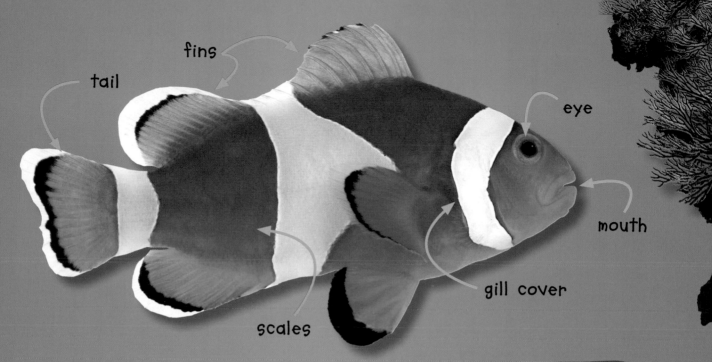

tail

fins

eye

mouth

gill cover

scales

↑ Clownfish are popular fish to keep in an aquarium.

Fish are animals that live and breathe in water. Some tanks in aquariums have fresh water in them, where fish from lakes, ponds and rivers live. Other tanks contain salt water, where fish and other animals from oceans and seas are kept.

Sea watch

SHARK HABITAT

ENDANGERED

The map shows where in the world the animal is from. Information about the most rare or at risk animals is given when you see the **endangered** symbol.

Sharks

Sharks are a kind of fish, but instead of scales on their body, they have a rough skin. Sharks find the smaller fish and other animals that they eat by smell and sight, or by tasting them in the water.

↓ A flesh-eating shark can have up to 3000 teeth in its mouth.

SHARK HABITAT

ZOO STARS

In 2009 a young sea lion jumped out of his enclosure at Pittsburgh Zoo, USA. It landed in the aquarium next door, which contained sharks. To the surprise of the keepers, the sharks ignored their visitor.

The smooth-hound sharks I saw were quite small, but some sharks are large. The biggest shark in the world is the whale shark, which can grow to more than 15 metres long and weigh up to 13 tonnes – that's as heavy as seven cars!

→ A hammerhead shark's eyes and nostrils are on the ends of its 'hammer'.

nostril

eye

The funniest-looking sharks I saw were called hammerhead sharks. They have a huge, flat head with eyes at the sides of it.

← The whale shark can grow to more than 15 metres. It eats tiny animals and plants.

Flat fish

Fish come in all shapes and sizes. Some fish, such as plaice and rays, have a thin, flat body.

MANTA RAY HABITAT

ENDANGERED

KLEIN'S SOLE
Location:
Mediterranean
Population:
Endangered —
very rare

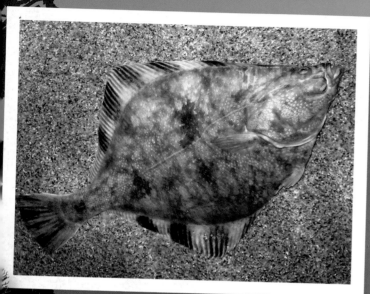

Plaice are flat fish. In the wild, plaice live close to the ocean floor. They can hide from their enemies by changing colour to blend in with the seabed. They swim on their sides.

← A flounder resting on sand.

→ A plaice buries itself in the sand to avoid being spotted by its enemies.

Rays also have a flat body. They swim using their huge fins like wings. The manta ray is the biggest ray in the world, but it only eats tiny water plants and animals.

The manta ray I saw was only I metre across, but it may grow to be 7 metres across. That's as long as one and a half cars!

← 7 metres across

↑ The manta ray swims through the sea like a giant bird.

ZOO VIEW

Plaice are an important food for human beings. In order to study where plaice swim in the sea, scientists in Suffolk, England, fitted plaice with electronic tags. The scientists discovered that a plaice can travel 900 kilometres in 56 days.

Sea horses

ENDANGERED
KNYSNA SEAHORSE
Location:
South Africa
Population:
Endangered —
world's rarest

Sea horses are fish that live in warmer seas. They swim upright and are covered in bony plates. Sea horses are tiny — most species are no more than 30 centimetres high.

→ no more than 10 centimetres high

↑ The sea horse gets its name because it swims upright and its head looks like a horse's.

ZOO VIEW

More than 25 million sea horses are sold as pets or to be made into medicines each year. A chocolate company in Belgium is paying scientists to find out more about sea horses and how they can be saved.

The sea horses I saw spent most of the time with their tails curled around seaweed. They were eating tiny shrimps and water plants that floated by them.

baby sea horse

male sea horse

↑ The sea horse is the only animal in the world in which the male gives birth to babies.

↑ Sea horses use their tails to hang on to weeds, not for swimming. They swim by waving their tiny fins.

When a female sea horse lays eggs, she puts them into a little pouch on the belly of the male sea horse. Between 10 days and 6 weeks later, more than 200 tiny sea horses hatch from the eggs and swim away from their father.

EEL HABITAT

ENDANGERED
YELLOW MARGIN
MORAY EEL
Location:
Pacific coast of
the Americas
Population:
Endangered

Eels

Although they have a long, thin body like snakes, eels are actually fish. They have fins on their backs and gills for breathing.

↓ The moray eel has a slimy, snake-like body. It only comes out of its hiding place at night to hunt for food.

The eels I saw were called moray eels. In the sea, moray eels hide in holes in rocks. They only come out at night to catch the shellfish they feed on.

The eels that live in lakes and rivers swim thousands of kilometres to the ocean, where they lay their eggs. About 3 years later, the young eels wriggle back into the rivers again. In some rivers in South America, the electric eel catches fish to eat by knocking them out with an electric shock.

↑ Freshwater eels swim huge distances from lakes and rivers far out into the Atlantic Ocean to lay their eggs.

Three things
you didn't know about...
EELS
1 There are about 600 kinds of eel living in fresh and salt water all over the world.

2 Young eels are called elvers.

3 The electricity produced by an electric eel is enough to shock a human being badly.

↑ The electric eel is actually a type of knife fish, not an eel, although it looks and swims like one.

ENDANGERED
MOSAIC REEF CRAB
Location:
Waters around
Singapore
Population:
Endangered —
very rare

Crabs and lobsters

Crabs and lobsters are not fish, even though they live in water. They are crustacean, so their body is covered with a hard shell that protects them from enemies.

As they grow, crabs and lobsters become too big for their shell. They have to shed the old shell so that a new, larger shell can grow.

↑ The boxer crab holds a sea anemone in each claw and waves their stinging tentacles at its enemies. The anemones eat the pieces of food the crab drops.

ZOO VIEW

Scientists in Australia are fixing concrete flowerpots to sea walls. The pots are new homes for crabs and other sea animals whose rock pool homes were destroyed when the walls were built.

→ Measuring up to 1 metre in length, the lobster uses its huge claws to crack open shellfish and feed on them at night.

Hermit crabs do not have their own shell. Instead, they live in the empty shell of another animal. The hermit crab I saw was living in the shell of a large **whelk**.

→ Hermit crabs mostly live on the seabed in warmer waters.

15

RARE
BLANKET OCTOPUS
Location:
Northern Australian
coast
Population:
Unknown

Octopuses and squid

The octopus is a sea animal with eight long arms, called tentacles. These tentacles have suckers on them that can grip prey tight. A squid is similar to an octopus, but has ten arms.

Sometimes octopuses walk along the seabed. They can also push themselves forwards with a jet of water that they shoot out of their body. If an octopus thinks it is in danger, it squirts thick black ink into the water. This hides the octopus while it escapes.

→ The suckers on an octopus's tentacles help the animal to grip its **prey** and to fasten itself onto rocks.

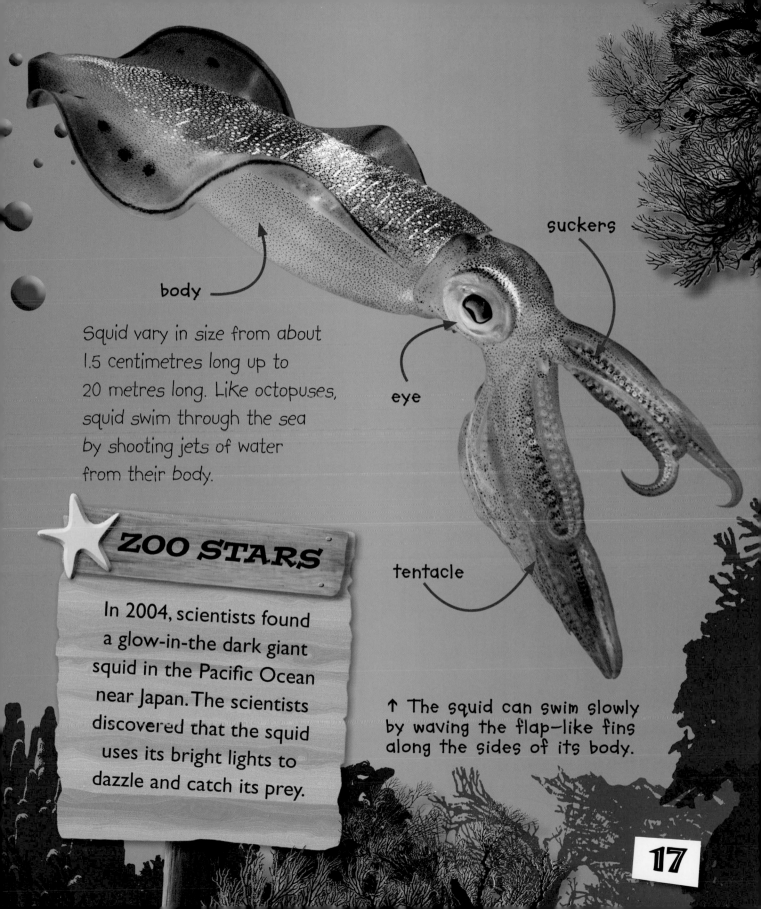

suckers

body

Squid vary in size from about
1.5 centimetres long up to
20 metres long. Like octopuses,
squid swim through the sea
by shooting jets of water
from their body.

eye

tentacle

ZOO STARS

In 2004, scientists found
a glow-in-the dark giant
squid in the Pacific Ocean
near Japan. The scientists
discovered that the squid
uses its bright lights to
dazzle and catch its prey.

↑ The squid can swim slowly
by waving the flap–like fins
along the sides of its body.

■ CORAL HABITAT

Corals

Although **corals** look like flowers, they are huge groups of tiny sea animals with shells. Corals are mostly found in warm, clear sea water where there is lots of light.

↓ A coral reef teems with beautiful and unusual animals.

The corals I saw in the aquarium were pink, orange and purple, but they come in other colours as well. Each tiny coral animal has stinging tentacles that stick out from its body. It uses these tentacles to catch tiny animals to eat.

→ Although they are animals, a lot of corals growing together look like an underwater garden.

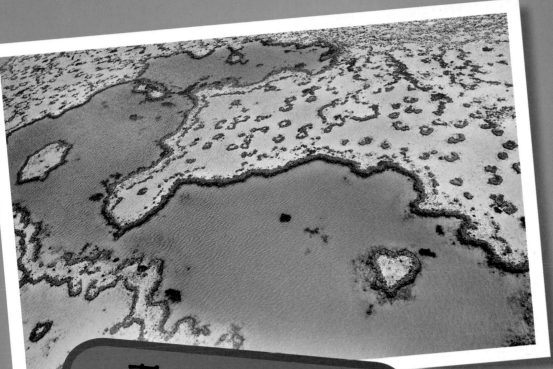

← A coral reef like this takes thousands of years to grow.

Three things
that will help...
CORALS

1 Sometimes shops near the sea sell pieces of coral as souvenirs. Don't buy these, because when coral is collected, it kills the animals inside.

2 Don't walk on a coral reef. Coral animals are easily damaged.

3 Don't spill suncream in the sea, because it might poison corals.

Thousands of years ago, corals formed rocky ridges called **reefs** on the seabed. Thousands of fish and other kinds of animals live in and around coral reefs. The reef shelters them and provides them with food.

Dolphins

Dolphins are intelligent, graceful animals. Although they are shaped like a large fish, dolphins are really mammals like us.

Fish can stay underwater all their life, but dolphins have to keep coming up to the surface to breathe air.

← This dolphin has a large number of small, sharp teeth to help it catch and eat fish.

■ DOLPHIN HABITAT

ENDANGERED
YANGTZE RIVER DOLPHIN
Location:
China
Population:
Less than 100

teeth

ZOO VIEW

Not all dolphins live in the sea. Some types live in rivers. The World Wide Fund for Nature, or WWF, has been working in Cambodia to save the dolphins that live in the Mekong River. It is believed there are fewer than 100 of these dolphins left.

← River dolphins are dolphins that have swum up from the sea and have begun living in rivers.

In the sea, dolphins live in groups. They swim near the surface, often jumping out of the water. They make clicking sounds and then listen for the **echoes** to bounce back from objects in the water. That is how they find their way and find the fish they eat.

↑ Dolphins often leap out of the water when they are playing.

↑ Dolphins feed their babies with milk from their body.

Glossary

Breed To produce babies.

Coral A hard substance built up from the seabed by tiny animals.

Echo A sound that bounces back and is heard again.

Endangered Describes an animal or plant that is in danger of becoming extinct.

Extinct Not existing anymore; when every one of a kind of animal or plant has died out.

Gill One of the parts of a water animal's body that it uses to breathe underwater.

Prey An animal that is hunted by other animals for food.

Reef A line of rock or coral just below or just above the surface of the sea.

Tentacle A long feeler, like a bendable arm.

Whelk A type of sea snail.

Index

Notes for parents and teachers

- Discuss with the children why it is necessary to be quiet and not run when visiting an aquarium. Why should you not tap on the glass in the tanks and why, in some aquariums, are you not allowed to use a camera with flash?

- Look through the book together. How many of the fish and other animals in the book can the children recognize?

- Most of the animals described in this book are fish, which are cold-blooded animals that have an internal skeleton and a backbone. Crabs, lobsters, octopuses and squid do not have an internal skeleton. Crabs and lobsters have an external shell, while octopuses and squid have no skeleton at all, but have a body that is supported by the water. Dolphins are warm-blooded mammals.

- Discuss with the children why some aquarium animals are in danger of becoming extinct. The main causes of extinction are overfishing, pollution and the destruction of the animals' natural habitat. In simple terms, overfishing is when fish are caught faster than they can breed and be replaced by more of the same species. If aquariums and zoos are able to breed endangered animals, they will not be able to release these animals into the wild unless a suitable safe place can be found for them.

- Explore movement and ask the children to move like an octopus, a crab or a dolphin.

- Introduce the children to the word 'camouflage'. Look at the book together. Which of the animals are camouflaged? What other animals can your child think of that are camouflaged?

- Do the children have a favourite kind of fish or aquatic animal? Why is this animal their particular favourite?

- Some useful websites for more information:

  www.nefsc.noaa.gov/faq

  www.bbc.co.uk/nature/animals

  www.kids.yahoo.com/animals

  www.zsl.org/education/

  www.nwf.org/wildlife

  www.thebigzoo.com

  www.arkive.org

  www.uksafari.com

  www.mcsuk.org

  www.panda.org